Studying *At the Cros*

CW00481711

Introduction

This photocopiable material offers classroom activities on *At the Crossroads*, from *Tracks 2*, the EDEXCEL anthology for GCSE English and English Literature*. It encourages pupils to engage actively with the texts, through close reading, role-play and discussion tasks. The logical progression through each text and the structured tasks ensure pupils are well prepared for the specific demands of the examination, able to develop their own coherent reading of the text. Rigorous critical analysis of language, form and meaning is complemented by opportunities for creative and imaginative writing, some of which are suitable for development as personal writing coursework for GCSE English.

The pupil chart on page 27 offers a structure for thinking about the audience, purpose and form of individual poetry texts. Activities on a sample pupil essay on pages 29-32 focus pupils on the particular demands of writing under exam conditions. The work on the poems of U.A. Fanthorpe and the assignments on page 28 provide pupils with the opportunity to practise comparing poems included in *At the Crossroads*, in preparation for question 1 in Papers 2F and 4H of the English examination. Questions suitable for exam practice are also included in the Writing/oral suggestions at the end of the work on each non-fiction text.

* *At the Crossroads* is prescribed for examination in GCSE English, Papers 2F/4H in 2002.

Acknowledgements

Thanks to Peter Ellison, Subject Leader at EDEXCEL for support and advice.
Thanks also to the following for permission to use copyright material: Penguin Books Ltd. for the typography, logo and layout of the front cover of *Cider With Rosie* and G. Lillicrap on behalf of Harold Harvey for *On the Way to Harvest*; Penguin Books Ltd. for approximately 400 words from 'St George and the Dragon' retold by Roger Lancelyn Green (adapted from *The Life of St. George* by Alexander Barclay, 1515) from *A Book of Dragons* edited by Roger Lancelyn Green (Puffin, 1970) © Roger Lancelyn Green; Jonathon Cape and Penguin Books Ltd. for the extract from *Boy* by Roald Dahl; Curtis Brown Ltd. London, on behalf of the Estate of Winston S. Churchill for *My Early Life* by Winston S. Churchill; The National Gallery for *Saint George and the Dragon* by Paolo Uccello.

Written by Lucy Webster
Editorial support: Lisa Hallgarten
Design: Eamonn England
Additional design: Fran Stowell
Publisher: English & Media Centre and EDEXCEL Foundation © 2000
ISBN: 0 90701668 5
Printed by Spider Web

Hide and Seek

Childhood games
- Spend a few minutes writing about your memories of playing outdoor and imaginative games as a child. Focus on one memory and try to capture the experience in words. Some of the things you could think about include:
- a description of the game
- who else played
- the place where you played
- the weather, the smells, the sounds you associate with this game
- your feelings when you lost and when you won.

- Working in pairs, share these memories and talk about the sections of your partner's writing which you find most powerful or enjoyable.

Fragments
Some key phrases and images from the poem have been re-printed for you here.
- Read through them carefully and consider the following points:
- what they suggest about the poem they are taken from
- the images they conjure up
- anything which you find surprising or striking.
  You could use drawings as well as words to explore your ideas.

| 'salty dark' | 'Hide in your blindness' | 'Their words and laughter scuffle' |

| 'The dark damp smell of sand moves in your throat' | 'The darkening garden watches' |

Reading the poem
- Read the poem once all the way through and jot down your first response. You could think about the story the poem tells, the character of the child, the presentation of childhood, the mood and the poet's use of language (sounds, word choices, images and so on).

- Get into groups and quickly share your ideas. Question any ideas you do not agree with and be prepared to defend your own interpretation by referring to the detail of the poem.

The tone and mood of the poem

- Without re-reading the poem, talk with your partner about what you feel the mood or tone of the poem is. Does it remain the same throughout the poem or does it alter?

- Now look back at the text of the poem. Identify the shifts in the tone and underline the words which suggest excitement and those which suggest threat. Some words to describe tone are suggested here:

| excited | proud | triumphant | tense | expectant | scared | anxious | frightened |

- As a class, talk about the way in which language and poetic techniques are used to create these shifts in tone. For example, is it through the sound of the words, the associations the reader has with the words used or the imagery?

The voice of the poem

The poem opens with an instruction ('Call out') and ends with a question ('But where are those who sought you?').
- What is the effect of this move from instruction to question?

The narrator of the poem seems to be talking to the child who is hiding in the 'toolshed', telling him what to do. The person giving the instructions could be any of the following people:
- the poet imagining the child hiding
- the child, now an adult, remembering what it was like to be that child playing hide and seek
- the child talking to himself.

- In pairs, talk about who you think the voice of the poem belongs to. Explain your ideas by referring to what is being said, how it is said and what it seems to be suggesting about childhood.

- Still working with your partner, prepare the poem as a script for reading aloud. Before you make your final decisions about how it should be said, practise reading it aloud in different ways. For example you could perform it as a dramatic reading with action, or use different voices for the descriptions, the instructions and the dialogue.

Exploring poetic techniques

This poem is very evocative. It conjures up for the reader the feelings of a child playing, as he moves from a feeling of triumph at the thought of winning, to the realisation that he has been abandoned by the others.
- Choose two or three phrases which seem to you to be particularly effective and make a few notes explaining your choices.

- Now look in more detail at the way Vernon Scannell uses language in these phrases and write a short paragraph exploring the language and poetic techniques. Some features of language to consider are suggested here:
- imagery, for example the personification used in 'The darkening garden watches'
- word choices, for example the description 'salty dark'
- sentence structures, for example the difference between the four short sentences in line 11 and the long sentence in lines 12 and 13.

The message of the poem

- Using the work you have completed on the development of the poem – the shifts in tone and so on – discuss, as a class, what you think the poem is saying about childhood.

Writing/oral suggestions
1. Your poem of childhood
Use 'Hide and Seek' as a model to help you write your own poem of childhood. You could use the notes you made on your memories of childhood games as the focus for your poem. Some techniques used by Vernon Scannell which you might like to experiment with are listed here:
– personification
– detailed focus on the five senses
– structuring the poem round the shifting tone (the move from anticipation and excitement through triumph and pride to fear and loneliness, for example)
– moving from a command to a question
– using an older narrator to set in context the experiences of the child.

2. A different medium
Re-write the poem in a different form, for example as the child's diary. Compare the original and the altered version making a note of the similarities and differences. Write a commentary exploring the advantages and disadvantages of each form.

3. A critical response
Explore Vernon Scannell's representation of childhood in the poem 'Hide and Seek' and the techniques he uses to create and communicate this image. Use the notes you made on the tone, language, imagery and voice of the poem as a starting point for planning your essay.

Half-past Two

Time to?

Although most people use clocks and watches to tell the time, many of us still use particular activities to divide up our day. At school, for example, we talk about play-time or break-time; at home we talk about tea-time and bedtime. These times are not shared by everyone: schools have their breaks at different times; even within the same family, people go to bed at different times. Imagine that we had no clocks to tell us the time in hours and minutes. What would you call the different parts of the day, or week or year? For example, what would you call the time between getting home from school and starting your homework? Would it be chatting-time, collapsing-time, telly-time ...?

- Use your imagination and re-name the day. Talk about what difference it would make to the way you think about each day. What would be the advantages and disadvantages of this sort of personal time?

The passing of time

- Working in pairs or small groups come up with a way of showing how particular times of the day seem to pass at different speeds depending upon what you are doing. For example, you could draw one time line to show the day divided into hours (clock-time) and one line to show how the passing of time feels to you.

- Present your ideas to the rest of the class.

The first line

- Before reading the whole poem, think about the expectations raised by the opening line.

> Once upon a schooltime

Hearing the poem

- Now listen to the poem being read out loud and jot down your first impressions. How far does the poem meet your expectations?

Exploring the characters

In the poem there are three characters – the narrator, the child and the teacher.

- Use different colours to highlight the thoughts, comments and speech of the three characters. Compare your work with the person next to you and talk about any sections you are uncertain about.

- In pairs, look more closely at the techniques U.A. Fanthorpe uses to distinguish the points of view of the different characters, for example capital letters, brackets, italics, word choices and imagery.

- What are your impressions of these three characters? Choose one, and describe this character in your own words. Annotate your description with short quotations from the poem to illustrate your interpretation.

A child's view of the world

Much of the power of this poem comes from U.A. Fanthorpe's ability to re-create a child's experience of the world.

- Look back at the poem and select three sections where you think U.A. Fanthorpe establishes the point of view of the child effectively. Work in pairs and talk about the techniques she uses to reflect this perspective. Think about:
- word choices

– presentation on the page, for example words running into each other
– sentence structure
– the representation of the world.

Capturing and escaping time – looking at the poetic techniques

The poem suggests that while adults' lives are ruled by time, children, who have not yet learned clock-time, are able to escape into a 'clockless land forever'. U.A. Fanthorpe uses the form and language of the poem to hold these ideas in tension.

• Working in small groups, identify the poetic techniques U.A. Fanthorpe uses both to represent the passing of time and to suggest the possibility of escaping the rules of time. Use the techniques listed here to get you started: repetition of words; sentence structures; the sound of the words; rhyme; rhythm; similes; metaphors and so on. You might find it helpful to read the poem out loud, tapping out the beat.

• Explore what each of the techniques you have identified contributes to the overall meaning of the poem and feedback your ideas in class discussion.

Lost time – reading the last verse

• Now read the final verse, re-printed for you here.

> But he never forgot how once by not knowing time,
> He escaped into the clockless land forever,
> Where time hides tick-less waiting to be born.

• Annotate the verse with your thoughts about the ideas it raises, for example, the image of time it presents. What does the poet seem to be suggesting about the way children and adults experience time?

A group reading of the poem

• Working in groups of three, prepare a reading of the poem, sharing out the parts so that your listeners hear the thoughts of the child, the asides of the narrator and the voice of the teacher. Use everything you have discussed about the themes and style of the poem to help you convey your interpretation of it.

• Enjoy listening to a few of the readings.

Writing/oral suggestions

1. A child's eye view

Using U.A. Fanthorpe's poem as a model, write about a different experience from the perspective of a child. Choose an event or incident which children and adults experience differently, or which a child might misunderstand (for example, Christmas or the birth of a new baby) and use your poem to make some comment on the differences between adults and children. You could experiment by using dialogue to show the two points of view and make up new words or ways of presenting words to capture the child's view.

2. Remembering childhood

Thirty years later the child in the poem, now a father, recalls this afternoon. He decides to write about his feelings then and now.

3. A critical response

Write an evaluation of the poem as an attempt to capture a child's experience of the world. You should think particularly about U.A. Fanthorpe's use of language, the layout and presentation of the poem and the use of three different points of view (the teacher, the child, the narrator).

Leaving School

Questions and expectations
- Before reading the poem look closely at the title and at the short fragment re-printed for you here.

> ... when I set out into the world
> wearing a grey flannel suit.

- What do you think the poem will be about? Who do you think is the speaker of the poem?

- Share your expectations with the rest of the class.

Over to you – setting out into the world
- Use the title and the first line to draft a short piece of writing of your own.

- Listen to some of these and talk about the similarities and differences in the way people have responded to the title and opening line. You should think about the following:
  - subject matter
  - voice
  - form (for example, notes, poem, letter)
  - point of view
  - tone and attitude
  - language.

Reading the poem
- Listen to 'Leaving School' being read out loud. Annotate your copy of the poem with anything which strikes you as interesting or surprising as you listen.

- Look back at the notes you made on your expectations of the poem. As a class talk about how far the poem met or challenged your early expectations. Why do you think Hugo Williams uses a title which creates such expectations?

Off to school – a boarding school experience
For anyone who has not been to boarding school, the rules and routines can seem strange and puzzling. There even seems to be a different language, for example 'prep' and 'half holidays'. In the two passages printed below, Winston Churchill and Roald Dahl describe their arrival at boarding school, remembering what it felt like to be left in a strange place at the age of seven.

- Read the extracts and in pairs talk about the similarities and differences between each passage and 'Leaving School'. You should think both about what the writer says and how he says it.

The fateful day arrived...

   The school my parents had selected for my education was one of the most fashionable and expensive in the country ... It was a dark November afternoon when we arrived at this establishment. We had tea with the Headmaster, with whom my mother conversed in the most easy manner. I was preoccupied with the fear of spilling my cup and so making 'a bad start'. I was also miserable at the idea of being left alone among all these strangers in this great, fierce, formidable place. After all I was only seven, and I had been so happy in my nursery with all my toys: a real steam engine, a magic lantern, and a collection of soldiers almost a thousand strong. Now it was to be all lessons every day except half holidays, and football or cricket in addition.

Winston Churchill: *An Early Life* (1930)

In September 1925, when I was just nine, I set out on the first great adventure of my life – boarding school. ... Every piece of clothing I wore was brand new and had my name on it. I wore black shoes, grey woollen stockings with blue turnovers, grey flannel shorts, a grey shirt, a red tie, a grey flannel blazer ... Into the taxi that was taking us to the docks went my brand new trunk and my brand new tuck-box, and both had R. DAHL painted on them in black.

A tuck-box is a small pinewood trunk which is very strongly made, and no boy has ever gone as a boarder to an English Prep School without one. ... At Prep School in those days, a parcel of tuck was sent once a week by anxious mothers to their ravenous little sons, ... An English school in those days was purely a money-making business owned and operated by the Headmaster. It suited him, therefore, to give the boys as little food as possible himself and to encourage the parents in various cunning ways to feed their off-spring by parcel post from home.

Roald Dahl: *Boy* (1984)

A child's experience

Although Churchill vividly describes the misery and confusion he felt as a child, he writes from the point of view of the adult looking back. As a result, his use of language is quite sophisticated. Even though Dahl's style is more straightforward, it is also written from the perspective of the adult explaining boarding school life. Hugo Williams, on the other hand, uses language to try and capture the point of view of the child. Some of the techniques he uses include:

– simple sentences
– capital letters in the middle of sentences (for example, Inspection)
– statements without explanations
– surprising or illogical connections between ideas
– snippets of things other people have told him.

- Make brief notes commenting on these techniques. Select short quotations from the poem to illustrate your analysis.

- Feedback your ideas in class discussion.

Filling in the gaps

To appreciate just how confused and lost the little boy feels as he tries to make sense of boarding school, the reader has to fill in the gaps in his story.

- Work in pairs. Read through the poem again, making a note of any questions you would like answered, for example, had he been told not to wear his outdoor shoes inside the school? What should he have been doing instead of 'walking around upstairs'?

- Next, using the poem and your questions, piece together the story of the narrator's first days away from home. You will need to think particularly carefully about the final verse.

Exploring the last line

The final words of the poem bring the reader back to the title, 'Leaving School', and to the picture of the boy with his suitcase.

- In pairs explore what you think is happening in the final line of the poem. For example, has the boy run away or is he day dreaming about leaving school? Share your ideas in class discussion.

- As a class talk about why you think Hugo Williams ends the poem with an echo of the opening lines. How effective an ending do you think it is? What does it add to the portrayal of boarding school life?

© Richard Greenhill

Writing/oral suggestions

1. A letter home

Children at boarding school were expected to write letters home to their parents. Write the letter which the little boy in 'Leaving School' might have written to his parents, describing his first experiences of life away from home.

2. A critical essay – snapshots from boarding school

Write a critical appreciation of the poem. You should think about:
– the picture presented of boarding school
– the voice of the poem
– the characterisation of the boy
– the structure of the poem
– the way language is used.

3. The poet speaks

Although this poem is written from the point of view of the child, the reader gets a clear sense of the poet's own views about boarding school. Imagine you are the poet giving a talk on 'Leaving School'. Explain what you wanted to show, the ideas or questions you wanted to raise and how you went about achieving this in poetry.

4. The mother replies

Write a reply to this poem in the form of a poem, monologue or letter from the point of view of the mother who has sent her child to school, aged eight years. You could explore her reasons for sending him; what she imagines he is doing and feeling on his first night away from home; her hopes for him and her worries about him.

Reports

The language of reports

- As a class spend a few minutes brainstorming all the typical words and phrases used in school reports. You might like to ask your parents and grandparents about their memories of comments often used on their school reports.

U.A. Fanthorpe's poem 'Reports' uses the clichés people associate with school reports. Listed below are all the phrases she presents as being possibilities for any teacher writing a report.
- Read through the phrases and talk about what each one really means. Do any of them seem surprising or out of place?

Has made a sound beginning	Satisfactory	Fair
Quite good	Unmanageable oaf	
Finds the subject difficult	Must make more effort	
Could have done better	Rest in peace	

Reading the poem – the first five verses

- Read the first five verses and share your ideas about the poem. Some things you might want to think about include:
- – what the poem is about
- – who is speaking
- – who is being spoken to ('you')
- – where you think the conversation is taking place
- – the tone of the poem (how you imagine the person giving the advice is speaking)
- – anything which strikes you about the way language is used.

Some good advice

The poem is presented as a series of instructions about how to write reports.

• Highlight the instructions and in pairs take responsibility for looking more closely at one of these. Annotate your verse with your response to the advice being given, your impression of the speaker and an exploration of the ways U.A. Fanthorpe creates this impression. Be prepared to feedback your ideas in class discussion. The example below shows you what to do.

Warning the teacher not to be too rude about the pupil – looks like the teacher is to blame.

All about looking as though doing the right thing in front of 'them'.

Be on your guard;
Unmanageable oaf cuts both ways.
Finds this subject difficult,
Acquitting you, converts
Oaf into idiot, usher to master.

Tone seems aggressive and defensive.

Legal language – makes it seem as though something is being fought over. Perhaps the 'them' in the poem might find the teacher guilty?

- After you have listened to the analyses of the first five verses, talk as a class, about the assumptions the speaker's advice makes about pupils, teachers and education.

The last two verses

- Now read the final two verses of the poem re-printed for you here.

> Remember your high calling:
> School is the world.
> Born at *Sound beginning*,
> We move from *Satisfactory*
> To *Fair*, then *Finds*
> *The subject difficult*,
> Learning at last we
> *Could have done better*.
>
> Stone only, final instructor,
> Modulates from the indicative*
> With *Rest in peace*.

* indicative – a sentence which states
a fact or asks a question.

- In pairs talk about your response to the last two verses. Use the points suggested here to help focus your thinking:
- who is speaking the last verses (is it the same character who has been giving the advice throughout the poem or someone else, for example, the poet?)
- the tone (for instance, is it confident, assertive, reflective, sad?)
- the intention of the person speaking
- the use of personal pronouns (I, you, they, we)
- the way in which the quotations from the reports are used in the last verses compared with the rest of the poem.

- On your own, re-read the whole of 'Reports'. Then, in pairs talk about whether knowing the final verses altered your response to the rest of the poem.

The language of the poem

This poem uses words and phrases from two specific areas – school and religion.
- Using two different colours highlight the language drawn from these areas.

- In pairs, or as a class, talk about the way in which, in the final verse, the poet brings together the language of school and religion to make a point about the way people go through life.

The message of the poem

- In no more than three sentences write down what you think the poem is about. In your opinion, what is U.A. Fanthorpe trying to get her readers to think about as a result of reading it? What attitudes, assumptions and prejudices is she challenging?

- After you have written down your own ideas, read through the statements listed here. Consider them carefully and, for each one, write a sentence explaining why you do or do not agree with it.

> U.A. Fanthorpe is critical of the way some teachers view pupils.

> This poem uses school as a metaphor or analogy for life.

> This poem is about both school and life.

> U.A. Fanthorpe is not critical of individual teachers but of the school system.

> U.A. Fanthorpe's criticism of the school system is really a criticism of the way many people treat life.

Writing/oral suggestions

1. A critical essay

In this poem school reports become a metaphor for a report on life. Write an essay exploring U.A. Fanthorpe's use of language and particularly this extended metaphor. You should comment on the way it is developed throughout the poem, particularly the shift between the early section of the poem and the last two verses.

2. Writing a poem

Develop your own extended metaphor for life, for example, a football game (kick-off, half-time, fouls, penalties and so on) or a journey. Use this as the central image in a poem exploring your attitude towards life or criticising the attitude you think other people have.

3. The teacher replies

In role as the teacher argue back to the narrator, presenting a more optimistic view of school and life in general. Use the points made in the different verses of the poem to help you structure your argument.

Dear Mr Lee

Laurie Lee and *Cider with Rosie*

Laurie Lee is the author of *Cider With Rosie*, a vivid and immediate description of his childhood growing up in the Cotswolds in the1920s. It is a book which has been relished by generations of readers since it was published in 1959; it is also a book which has frequently been studied for examination. The second part of his autobiography, *As I Walked Out One Midsummer Morning*, is an account of his involvement in the Spanish Civil War of 1936 – 1939.

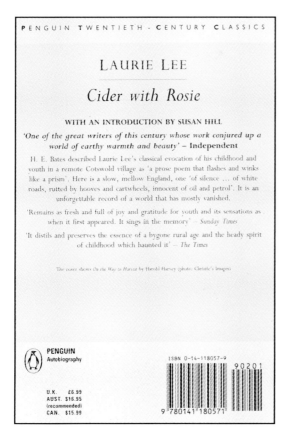

Reading the poem
- Enjoy listening to the poem being read aloud and, as a class, talk about your response to the narrator and the opinions she expresses.

The form of the poem
The presentation and layout of 'Dear Mr Lee' is very different from the other poems you have read so far in *At the Crossroads*.
- Work in pairs and make a list of everything you notice about the way the poem is presented on the page. Choose a quotation to illustrate each of your observations. An example is given to get you started.

Form	Quotation	Comment
Irregular line length	*'but that's how I think of you having lived with you nearly all year). Dear Mr Lee'*	*Makes it seem hurried.*

- As a class, talk about what the form contributes to the overall impact of the poem.

The voice of the narrator

In this poem the reader gets a full picture of what the speaker is like both through what she says and how she says it. The language and the structure of the poem reflect the chatty informal tone of the spoken voice.

- Pull out some of the phrases which suggest this chatty informality and talk about what impression they give of the speaker.

As well as the pupil's voice, two other voices can be heard clearly in the poem: the teacher and the examiner.

- Highlight two or three examples of these two characters speaking through the pupil, for example, 'a character-sketch/Of your mother under headings'. Annotate your choices with what it is which identifies these as belonging to an adult voice, for example, vocabulary, tone, attitude, sentence structure and so on.

Whose Laurie Lee is it anyway?

The reader of 'Dear Mr Lee' is presented with different attitudes towards both *Cider With Rosie* and Laurie Lee himself.

- Look back over the poem and jot down a few notes on the views and attitudes the different characters have towards Laurie Lee and *Cider With Rosie*.

- Next, writing in role, explain each character's attitude towards reading literature for examination. Share these in small groups and talk about how different people have conveyed the attitudes explored in the poem.

A mini-debate

- Working in pairs, take responsibility for preparing the argument in favour of one of the following statements:
- Studying literature spoils enjoyment of it.
- Studying literature improves understanding and therefore appreciation of it.

- Join up with another pair who have worked on the other argument and present your case.

You could develop this work into a piece of written coursework or a speaking and listening assignment.

Writing/oral suggestions
1. The examiner speaks

One way of reading this poem is as a criticism of exams which force students to write tidy, acceptable essays, without taking their emotional response into account. It may seem strange therefore that you are being asked to study this poem for an exam. Imagine you are the examiner who had to convince U.A. Fanthorpe to agree to her poems being set for GCSE examination. What do you say? Why is it important to study poetry at school?

2. A letter to U.A. Fanthorpe

Write a letter to U.A. Fanthorpe describing your response to her poem. You can write about the poem in any way you choose. This is a good opportunity to ask questions or explain what you find difficult about the poem. You could also refer to any other poems by U.A. Fanthorpe included in *At the Crossroads*.

3. A comparison

Look back at your notes on U.A. Fanthorpe's poem 'Reports'. Write an essay discussing the way in which school is presented in both poems. You should also consider the way in which the poet uses school to explore wider themes and issues, for example, the relationship between adults and children.

You will be hearing from us shortly

What sort of poem looks like this?

- Spend a few minutes talking as a class about the layout of the poem, represented in the diagram below.

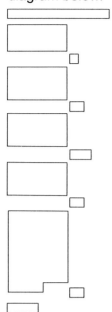

What sort of conversation?

- Look closely at the phrases in the boxes. They are taken from the right hand side of the poem. In pairs talk about the tone of voice you imagine they would be said in.

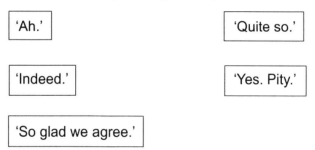

Improvising the conversation

- Working in pairs, use the fragments taken from the poem to improvise the conversation you think they belong to. Use these questions as prompts to get you started.

  - What sort of conversation do you think they are taken from?
  - Where do you think this conversation takes place?
  - What do you imagine the speaker to be like?
  - What about the person whose comments have provoked these responses?

- Listen to a few of the conversations, making notes on the different ways in which people used the fragments. Think about:
  - subject matter
  - tone
  - the relationship between the two people (For example, was it obvious who had most authority? If so, how could you tell?)
  - the way in which the conversation developed (Did it, for example, become more or less friendly as it progressed).

- Feedback your discoveries in class discussion and talk about the main similarities and differences.

Exploring the title

- As a class quickly share your response to the title, 'You will be hearing from us shortly'. Where would you expect to hear this phrase? What do you think it means?

Reading the poem

- Listen to U.A. Fanthorpe's poem being read out loud one verse at a time. After each verse has been read, make a note of your reaction and jot down any of the words or phrases which affected you particularly strongly.

- Once you have heard the whole of 'You will be hearing from us shortly', look back over both the poem and your notes on your developing response. At what point did you first become uneasy? Why was this?

- As a class share your thoughts on the poem and your reaction to it. Concentrate on any sections which caused you to sit up and listen a bit more closely.

The interviewer

- Identify everything which, in the opinion of the interviewer, is wrong with the applicant. Are any of the reservations the interviewer expresses about the applicant reasonable ones? If so, at what point do these become unreasonable?

As the poem progresses, the prejudices of the interviewer become more explicit. In the first verse the criticism of the applicant is subtle: 'You feel adequate to the demands of this position?'; by the final verse the interviewer voices his/her criticism openly and in what most people would consider to be unacceptable terms: 'The usual desire to perpetuate what had better not have happened at all'.

- Highlight the attitudes which are offensive or discriminatory. Next, annotate the poem to show how this attitude is revealed in the language of the poem, for example in the word choices, the silences, the structure of the sentences, the use of questions and so on.

- Feedback your ideas to the class and talk about the way in which U.A. Fanthorpe manages to indicate her own disapproval of these attitudes.

The applicant speaks

Although we hear only one side of the conversation, it is easy to work out the type of thing the applicant might say, and even to speculate about the way in which it is said.
- Working on your own, annotate a copy of the poem with speech bubbles showing the other side of the conversation.

It is unlikely that this applicant said what he or she wanted to in this interview.
- Go through the poem for a second time and add thought bubbles in which the applicant argues with the interviewer, challenging their prejudices.

Language and power

- Read the poem again, imagining the expression of the speaker and the way he or she looks – or doesn't look – at the applicant at different points. How do you think the correction in line 26 is said ('We mean, of course,/Where were you educated?')? If possible, read the poem out loud.

- As a class share your impressions of the speaker. How would you describe the way they speak and use language? For example is it friendly, intimate and chatty, or distant and formal?

The use of standard English, complex sentences and the first person plural ('we') gives the speaker of this poem an air of authority; the way he or she uses language helps suggest that what they are saying is the truth, giving credibility to their opinions.

- Identify a quotation which strikes you as characteristic of the way this person speaks, and which seems to convey their attitude towards the applicant and his/her social background. Share your thoughts on the section you have chosen and try to identify what helps create this impression. Some of the language features you should think about are suggested here:
  - vocabulary
  - sentence structures (Have a look at the order of words in sentences like the one in lines 19-21)
  - rhetorical questions
  - use of pronouns ('We' and 'us' against 'You').

Critical views

As with all good poems there are different ways of interpreting 'You will be hearing from us shortly.' Some possible interpretations of the poem are listed here.

- This poem begins in a realistic way but becomes surreal.
- The verses on the left-hand side are what the interviewer thinks but does not say.
- This poem includes all the prejudices an applicant might come across in an interview.
- U.A. Fanthorpe exaggerates in order to make a point about interviewers.
- This poem is about prejudice.
- This poem is not about prejudice; it is about power relationships.
- It is a poem about the way some people abuse their position of power.
- It shows how close some interviewers come to breaking the boundaries of what is acceptable.
- It makes us think about the opinions which we often accept without thinking.
- It is a spoof interview, a joke, not meant to be taken seriously.

- On your own, read through the statements about the poem, ticking those you agree with. Add any other ideas you have about the poem and what it might be about.

- In pairs, compare the decisions you made. Then using the statements you agree with as a starting point, share your interpretation of the poem in class discussion.

Writing/oral suggestions

1. A critical essay

Write a short essay describing your impressions of the speaker of this poem and explaining how the poet creates this impression. You should think about the layout and presentation, the tone, the language and the decision to include only the thoughts and/or comments of the interviewer.

2. A letter from the applicant

In role as the applicant, write a letter to the interviewer explaining why you think the interview was unfair. Briefly outline your interpretation of the interviewer's comments before exploring their opinions in more detail. Use the verses of the poem to help you structure your argument.

3. A one sided poem

Use the form of U.A. Fanthorpe's poem as a model for a poem of your own. Choose another situation where the relationship between the people involved is not equal, for example, headteacher and pupil, parent and child or doctor and patient. Write the questions and responses of *either* the person who holds the power *or* the person who is being intimidated. Your reader should get a strong impression of the speaker's character and be able to work out something about the other side of the conversation.

Telephone conversation

A conversation extracted

This poem is built around a telephone conversation between two people who have never met before. Part of the dialogue has been extracted for you.

- Read the dialogue all the way through once. What do you think is going on in this conversation?

> – Madam, I hate a wasted journey – I am African.
> – HOW DARK? ARE YOU LIGHT OR VERY DARK? ARE YOU DARK? OR VERY LIGHT?
> – You mean – like plain or milk chocolate? West African sepia. Down in my passport.
> – WHAT'S THAT? DON'T KNOW WHAT THAT IS.
> – Like brunette.
> – THAT'S DARK, ISN'T IT?
> – Not altogether. Facially, I am brunette, but madam, you should see the rest of me.

- Next, in pairs work through the dialogue again, this time annotating it with your ideas. Some things for you to think about are suggested here:
- what you think the conversation is about
- who is speaking
- the relationship between the two people
- their attitude towards each other
- any themes which you think are being explored.

The whole poem

- Listen to the whole of 'Telephone Conversation' being read out loud and make a note of your reaction.

- Share your first thoughts about the poem with the rest of the class.

This poem was written when the poet came to London, as a student, in the 1960s. Since then it has been included in many anthologies. It is now one of Soyinka's most famous poems. It is difficult to imagine what it must have felt like to experience, on a daily basis, casual, open racism of the sort presented here. At the time when the poem was written, and even when it was first published in 1976, the attitudes expressed by the landlady were common and widely accepted.

Reading the poem

The speaker of the poem is in an old fashioned telephone box. In these phone boxes the person in the telephone box had to press button A in order to speak to the person when they answered.

- Work in groups of three and prepare a dramatic reading of the whole poem. One of you could read the thoughts and comments of the narrator; the other two could read the dialogue of the characters. Read the poem all the way through to yourself before you start to talk about how you will dramatise it. You will need to think about:
- tone of voice of each character at different points in the poem
- pace
- pauses and silences
- gestures and body language
- relationship between the narrator and the listener.

- Listen to a few of the readings and talk about the different ways in which the groups have presented the conversation and which aspects they have chosen to emphasise.

Exposing prejudice

Wole Soyinka uses the particular features of a telephone conversation in order to expose the unthinking racial prejudice of people like the landlady.

• As a class talk about the techniques the poet uses to highlight the racism in the landlady's attitude.

Exploring the language and structure of the poem

Listed below are some words to describe the feelings of the narrator at different points in the poem.

angry	disbelieving	resigned	shocked	amused	bitter

• Skim read the poem again and choose what you think are the most appropriate descriptions. Label the different sections of the poem with these descriptions and make a note of the reasons for your decision.

Some of the language features and poetic techniques used by Soyinka to convey these feelings are listed below.

• For each one write a sentence exploring how you think this technique is used in the poem and find a quotation to illustrate your comment.
– the use of colour
– the repetition of single words (such as red)
– dialogue
– rhythm
– the combination of long sentences with very short ones
– questions
– capital letters
– the absence of the definite article (the).

The tone of the poem

The poem deals with a serious subject. It is an excellent example of the power of words to confront and challenge people's assumptions and prejudices. The tone, however, is not uniformly sombre. One of the weapons Soyinka uses against prejudice, for example, is wit and humour.

• Identify examples of humour in the poem and talk about how effective you think it is as a way of fighting racism.

Writing/oral suggestions
1. A critical essay

Write a short critical essay on the poem commenting on the ideas it raises and analysing the way in which these are explored. Describe the ways in which Soyinka uses the poem as a means of confronting and challenging prejudice.

2. A letter home

Wole Soyinka wrote this poem when studying in London. Draft the letter he may have written to his family describing the prejudice he encountered.

3. A poem exploring prejudice

You too may have experienced prejudice in some form, whether this is because of your age, class, race or something else. Write a poem in which you attempt to convince someone to treat you as an individual.

Not My Best Side

The title
- As a class, brainstorm everything the title 'Not My Best Side' makes you think of, for example, who might say it, what sort of voice it might be said in, the circumstances someone might say it in and so on. What sort of poem do you think would have a title like this?

The painting *St. George and the Dragon*
- Now look closely at this picture. It was painted by the Italian artist Paolo Uccello in the second half of the fifteenth century.

Saint George and the Dragon by Paolo Uccello, reproduced with the permission of The National Gallery, London

- What impression do you get of the characters? What image do you think the artist wants to present? Identify the parts or features of the painting which make you think this.

- Share your ideas in small groups and talk about the similarities and differences in the way people have interpreted the painting.

Telling the story
- Working in fours, take turns to tell the story of what is happening in the picture, using the voice of one of the characters. One of you could try and tell it from the point of view of an unseen observer.

The story of St George and the dragon
- As a class, share everything you know about the story of St. George and the dragon. Talk about the plot of the story, the characters involved, and the way this story and these characters have been used in other situations. (For example, St George has been recognised as the patron saint of England from the days of Edward III in the thirteenth century.)

• Now read the version of the story of George and the Dragon printed here. It is taken from *A Book of Dragons,* edited by Roger Lancelyn Green (Penguin, 1970).

> 'The Dragon rages for his food – and our children perish. Let your daughter be given to him as our sons and daughters have been.'
>
> Then the King arrayed Princess Sabra in wedding garments as if the day of her nuptials had come. And he kissed her and blessed her, and afterwards led her to the place where the Dragon was wont to come for his horrible meals and left her there.
>
> As she stood weeping and shivering with fear, waiting for the Dragon, she heard the sound of horse's hooves and the clink of armour – and George of Cappadocia came riding by with his sword at his side and a spear in his hand.
>
> 'Fair lady,' said he, 'why do you stand here in bridal array, weeping so sorely?'
>
> 'Do not stop to ask, fair young man, but ride for your life or you will perish also,' cried Sabra.
>
> 'I do not stir until you tell me of the danger and why you wait here alone to face it,' he answered gravely.
>
> Seeing that he would not go, Sabra told him of the Dragon, and of how he might be expected at any moment to come and carry her off.
>
> Then said George of Cappadocia: 'Fair lady, fear no more. For I shall save you by the grace of Jesus Christ.'
>
> 'By your gods and mine, fly swiftly, noble knight,' she begged. 'No one may save me and you will only share my fate.'
>
> Even as she spoke, the reeds by the lake began to rustle, a dark smoke rose suddenly above them, and the Dragon burst into sight and came rushing hungrily towards them.
>
> Then George leapt upon his horse, made the sign of the cross, and commending himself to God and Our Saviour set his spear in rest and charged the Dragon. So true and strong was his aim that the spear went through the monster's throat and deep into its body, and it stopped in its course and fell upon its side, grievously hurt.
>
> George sprang from his horse, drew his sword and lashed at the Dragon, wounding it again so that it laid its head on the ground, quite overcome.
>
> 'Lady,' said the knight, 'take off your girdle and bind it about the head of the Dragon. Do not be afraid, it will not hurt you now.'
>
> Then Sabra did as he bade; and when she had fastened her girdle to the Dragon it followed her like a tame beast.

• Compare your stories of the painting with both what you know about the story of St. George and the version printed here. Talk about the similarities and differences, focusing your discussion on the following points:
- the plot (what happens)
- the characters involved and the way they are represented
- the themes
- the values and beliefs upheld and/or challenged by the story.

The poem 'Not My Best Side'
U.A. Fanthorpe's poem 'Not My Best Side' is based on this painting.
• Before you read the poem, look back at the notes you made on the title and think for a few minutes about the relationship between the painting and her choice of title for the poem.

A poem in three voices
• Work in groups of three. Each group will be given responsibility for reading one of the verses of the poem. Read your verse and on your own jot down your impressions of the character.

• Share your first thoughts with the other people in the group, then spend a few minutes reading your verse out loud, experimenting with different tones and expressions.

- Now talk in more detail about the character U.A. Fanthorpe has created. Some points you might like to think about are suggested below:
  - the character's views on the way they have been presented by the artist
  - the way the characters see themselves
  - the voice of the character
  - the way this character and voice has been created (for example, word choices, sentence structures and so on).

Writing/oral suggestions
1. The poet and artist in conversation
A speaking and listening assignment for two pupils

Imagine the poet U.A. Fanthorpe meets the painter of the picture she wrote about. One person play the part of the poet, the other person play the part of the painter. In role, jot down the questions you would like to ask the other artist about their representation of the story of St. George and the dragon. Swap questions and spend a few minutes preparing your answers. Then improvise their conversation.

A writing assignment for individual work

U.A. Fanthorpe and Uccello, the painter, are both invited to speak about their work on the BBC Arts programme on Radio 4, *Front Row*. Write the transcript of the discussion they have. You might find it helpful to invent a presenter to act as interviewer or chair of the discussion.

2. The poet's intention

> In 'Not My Best Side' U.A. Fanthorpe challenges the traditional, stereotypical characters in the legend of St. George and the dragon only to replace them with another equally stereotypical set.

Use this statement as the starting point for writing critically about what you think U.A. Fanthorpe tried to do in this poem.

Before tackling this essay, you might find it helpful to work through the activities suggested here.
- As a whole class, talk about which characters are presented in a favourable light in the stories of St. George and the dragon which you shared earlier. Consider whether this is also true of U.A. Fanthorpe's poem.

- Listed below are some statements on the possible message of the poem. Read them all carefully and, bearing in mind your discussions, tick the ones you agree with.

  - This poem challenges stereotypes.
  - This poem creates new stereotypes.
  - U.A. Fanthorpe uses humour to make a serious point.
  - The poet wants to make the characters from legend seem like real people.
  - She uses the characters from legend to comment on relationships between men and women today.
  - She is critical of the painter's representation of the story.
  - She shows that even if people want to be different, they cannot escape 'the roles/That sociology and myth have designed' for them.

- For each statement you choose, write a couple of sentences commenting on the view expressed. You should explain as fully as you can why you think it can be supported by a reading of the poem.

Old Man, Old Man

Before reading

- Work in groups of four. One pair work on the extracts re-printed in Box A, the other pair work on those in Box B. Based on these extracts, write a short description of the person they might refer to.

Box A	Box B
his hands shamble among clues	pictures of disinherited children
you ramble/In your talk	Your surliness
fretting	world authority
your contracted world	Lord
living in almost dark	adjuster of environments
you tried not to cry	timetabled cigarette
Your helplessness	A man who did-it-himself
	not good with daughters

Reading the poem

- Listen to verses 1 to 9 being read to you, recording your response as you listen.

- Now you know that the sets of fragments describe the same man, does it alter your view of him? How do you think the narrator sees him? Make a note of your own reaction and any ideas you have about the narrator's attitude towards the man now (Box A), and in the past (Box B).

A changing relationship

• Now read the final lines of the poem re-printed for you here

Old man, old man,
So obdurate in your contracted world,
Living in almost-dark, *I can see you*

You said to me, *but only as a cloud*.
When I left, you tried not to cry. I love
Your helplessness, you who hate being helpless.

Let me find your hammer. Let me
Walk with you to Drury Lane. I am only a cloud.

These lines alter the way in which we read the rest of the poem. It no longer seems to be just about the man, but about his relationship with the narrator.

- What do these lines suggest about the relationship between these two people in the past? How has it changed? What does the narrator hope it will be like in the future?

Looking for patterns

The poem explores the changing relationship between the narrator and a man, possibly her father. The changes brought about by the man growing older are conveyed through U.A. Fanthorpe's use of oppositions, for example, the past and the present.

- Use two different colours to highlight the sections of the poem which describe the past and those which refer to the present.

Some more oppositions used in the poem are suggested here:
- words to do with control and weakness
- words to do with authority and incompetence
- memories and descriptions of the present
- poetic and colloquial (or everyday) language
- descriptions of feelings and descriptions of objects
- thoughts and speech
- references to the old man in the third person (he) and the second person (you)

- As a class add any other oppositions you have noticed in the poem.

- Work in pairs and take responsibility for one of these oppositions. Begin by identifying words and images which belong to the pair of opposites you are working on. Then explore in detail the way this opposition is used in the poem. Do you notice any patterns? Is the pattern ever broken? What insight does this opposition give you into the themes or meaning of the poem? Present your ideas to the rest of the class. An example is given here to show you the sort of thing you might say.

The words to do with authority are mainly associated with the man and are found in the sections of the poem describing the past. The words to do with weakness refer mainly to the old man – what he has become in the present. They suggest he is no longer the powerful, authoritative – perhaps frightening – figure he once was. He is now dependent on his daughter who loves his 'helplessness'. However, the repetition of the word 'Let' in the final verse makes it sound as though she is still having to plead to be allowed to do anything to help.

Writing/oral suggestions
1. A critical response

> This poem is about the narrator's relationship with someone who has grown old.

Write a short critical essay commenting on the poem in the light of this statement. How far do you think it is an adequate summary of the poem? What do you think it is about? You should base your analysis of the poem on a close and detailed reading.

2. A video poem
Plan and write notes for a video poem of 'Old Man, Old Man'. Some points you should think about include:
- mood/tone
- point of view
- how you will tell the story of the man's life (in flashback? chronologically?)
- how you will show the relationship between the old man and the narrator now and in the past
- how you will represent the imagery in visual form.

3. A conversation
Work in pairs and improvise a conversation in which this man and the narrator talk about the way their relationship has changed over the years. Remember that each will have a very different view of the relationship. For example, did the man realise he was not 'good with daughters'? Perhaps the narrator of the poem always seemed to look down on his DIY, not realising it was his attempt to look after his family.

Warning

Growing older
- Before you read Jenny Joseph's poem, jot down some notes under the following headings:
- – your views of old people (positive and negative)
- – your positive expectations of what it will be like to grow old
- – your anxieties about growing old
- – what you think you will be like as an old person (what you will do, your attitudes and so on).

- In pairs or as a class, share some of your thoughts and feelings.

Reading the poem
- Read the poem to yourself. As you read, try and hear the voice of the speaker – you might find it helpful to read the poem aloud or under your breath.

- Jot down your first response to the poem. Use the questions suggested here as a starting point.

- – Did you enjoy the poem? If so, why?
- – What impression do you have of the speaker?
- – What do you think the poet is saying both about adulthood and about old age?

A dramatic reading
- Work in pairs and prepare a dramatic reading of the poem. Some of the things you will need to consider include:
- – tone
- – pace
- – expression
- – gestures and body language
- – your relationship with your audience.

- As you practise reading the poem aloud, be alert to the way that Jenny Joseph directs you through her use of rhythm, rhyme and the structure and length of her sentences. Annotate the poem with anything you notice as you go along. You may find it helpful to record your reading so that you can listen to the way in which the sound of the poem is used to reflect its meaning.

- Enjoy listening to a few of the dramatic readings. Then share your thoughts on the techniques Jenny Joseph uses to convey her feelings about the way in which people are expected to behave.

The voice of the poem
- Based on the readings you have heard and on the discussions you have had, write a paragraph describing the voice of the poem and explaining how Jenny Joseph uses this voice to challenge the reader's assumptions. Begin by thinking about how you would describe the tone in which the speaker voices her plans for the future. What sort of relationship is built up with the reader? Are we kept at a distance or invited to share her rebellion?

A middle aged rebellion?
The poem 'Warning' is about behaving in a rebellious way.
- What is the speaker of the poem rebelling against? Make a list of the ways in which she is expected to behave now. You could express these as a series of commands, for example, 'Women must not wear bright colours'.

- What image of society is presented in the poem? Of the restrictions she is going to rebel against, which seem reasonable and which, if any, should not exist at all? Write up your notes into a short paragraph outlining the points Jenny Joseph makes in the poem.

The title

- Why is it called 'Warning'? Who do you think it is a warning for or about?

Writing/oral suggestions

1. Beware

Jenny Joseph writes about the freedom of being old, when people will stop expecting her to behave in a responsible manner. Another time when people experience freedom from restrictions and the expectations of others is when they leave home for the first time, often to go away to college. Follow Jenny Joseph's example and write your own poem about what you will do when you first experience this freedom.

2. The nation's favourite.

Since 1995 the BBC has conducted a poll for National Poetry Day to find the Nation's Favourite Poem. In 1995 Jenny Joseph's 'Warning' was voted number 17 – the highest position for a living poet. In 1997 people were asked to name their favourite twentieth century poem; 'Warning' was voted number 1.

Imagine it is National Poetry Day 1997. You have been asked to go on the BBC's arts programme on Radio 4 to talk about the results of the poll. Choose one of the following roles and prepare your notes for the discussion:

- a poetry lover who voted for 'Warning'
- a critic who thinks another poem should have won
- Jenny Joseph.

3. A critical essay

Write a critical essay analysing the way Jenny Joseph uses the language and the structure of the poem to convey both her excitement at her plans for growing old and her frustration at the way she is expected to behave now. Look back at the notes you made when preparing your dramatic presentation to help you prepare your essay. Some language features you should think about are suggested here:

- beginning lines with 'And'
- the length of sentences
- using non-standard or childish English, for example, 'grow more fat'
- the division of the poem into the different stanzas
- the question in the final verse
- the different effects of using 'shall' (verse 1), 'can' (verse 2) and 'must' (verse 3)
- the circular structure of the poem.

Comparing poems

Poem	Subject	Themes	Point of view/ voice	Tone	Language	Relationship with the reader/effect on the reader	Presentation
Hide and Seek							
Half-past Two							
Leaving School							
Reports							
Dear Mr Lee							
You will be hearing from us shortly							
Telephone Conversation							
Not My best Side							
Old Man, Old Man							
Warning							

You may find it helpful to enlarge this chart to A3

The poems of U.A. Fanthorpe

Thinking about a poet
The anthology *At the Crossroads* includes five poems by a single poet, U.A. Fanthorpe.
- Re-read these poems and jot down anything you notice about them which seems to you characteristic of her poetry (for example, the subject, themes, style or tone). Choose short quotations to illustrate each of the points you want to make.

- In class discussion compare your views of U.A. Fanthorpe's poetry. What aspects and features of the poems have different people focused on?

Critical reviews
The quotations printed below are taken from reviews of U.A. Fanthorpe's work. They give some idea of what other critics think are the characteristic concerns and features of her poetry.

- Read the quotations carefully, ticking those you agree with.

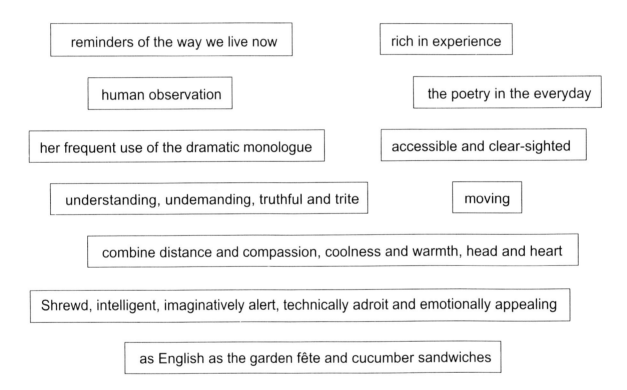

> reminders of the way we live now

> rich in experience

> human observation

> the poetry in the everyday

> her frequent use of the dramatic monologue

> accessible and clear-sighted

> understanding, undemanding, truthful and trite

> moving

> combine distance and compassion, coolness and warmth, head and heart

> Shrewd, intelligent, imaginatively alert, technically adroit and emotionally appealing

> as English as the garden fête and cucumber sandwiches

- Write a sentence explaining why you think the comments you have ticked are true of U.A. Fanthorpe's poetry. For each one, choose a short quotation from one or more of the poems to support what you are saying.

Writing about poetry in the exam

Twentieth century poetry in *At the Crossroads*

In the English examination you will be asked to write about two of the poems included in your anthology, *At the Crossroads*. This question will test your reading, particularly your ability to:
- show sustained interpretation of content, language and presentation
- read with insight and engagement
- make appropriate references to the text.

You will be asked a question on either two of the poems by U.A. Fanthorpe or one poem by U.A. Fanthorpe and a further poem by one of the other poets included in the anthology. The poems you have to write about may be named or you may be given a free choice. It is a good idea to think about which poems you might compare before you go into your English exam. Some ideas are suggested here:
- 'Old Man, Old Man' and 'Warning'
- 'Half-past Two' and 'Leaving School'
- 'Half-past Two' and 'Hide and Seek'
- 'Not My Best Side' and 'Telephone Conversation'.

Writing to time

Before your exam it is a good idea to practise writing timed essays. Use this general question as a focus for writing about any two of the poems.

> **Write in detail about the experience explored in the poems, commenting on what you have found interesting in the poet's use of language.**

Some points you should think about when writing about any of the poems in the collection:
- the presentation of the subject matter
- point of view
- the structure
- tone
- language (images, comparisons, descriptions, words or phrases which you find particularly effective)
- the layout and appearance of the poem on the page.

A pupil essay

Preparing for the exam – Wole Soyinka: 'Telephone Conversation'

Before trying this exercise, re-read the poem 'Telephone Conversation' and remind yourself of the work you have already completed on it.

Writing a timed essay

As part of their exam preparation, a class of pupils was asked by their teacher to have a go at answering the following question, under timed conditions.

> **Describe the ways in which Wole Soyinka uses 'Telephone Conversation' as a means of confronting and challenging prejudice.**

Exploring the question

- Read the question underlining or highlighting what you consider to be the most important words. Make a note of what you are being asked to write about in your answer.

- Talk about your ideas with a partner and come up with a plan for the essay.

- Feedback your ideas in class discussion and talk about how you would go about tackling this question in the exam.

A first attempt

- Have a go at answering this question in exam conditions. You should spend between five and ten minutes thinking and planning your answer, about thirty minutes writing and save five minutes for reading and checking.

A pupil essay

The essay printed below was written under timed conditions by a Year 11 pupil. It is reproduced here exactly as the pupil wrote it.

- Read the essay carefully and, in pairs, talk about how it compares to your own first attempt at answering the question.

This poem raises ideas about racial prejudice. These ideas are explored by using the format of a telephone conversation to express the hidden prejudices of the landlady. Tension is created early in the poem when the poet says 'I hate a wasted journey – I am African.' He says this as if he expects the worst. It implies that he has been turned down in the past, for that exact reason. The use of the term 'self confession' makes it seem as if race is something to be ashamed of. The description of silence at the other end says a lot about the reaction of the landlady; the 'silenced transmission of pressurised good breeding' suggests that she is very uncomfortable with the situation, and is trying to hide her prejudices by 'good breeding'. When she asks the question 'How dark?' both the poet and the reader are shocked. Surely prejudice is prejudice and asking for an exact description of his colouring is even more degrading than if the woman had just said yes or no. It magnifies the prejudice by trivialising it, as if it matters 'how dark' he is.

The poet is dumbfounded and feels shame and humiliation at the question. The landlady replies as if the poet is stupid, patronises him as if what she has just asked him is a perfectly standard question, 'Are you dark or very light?'. The description of her 'clinical assent' 'crushing in its light impersonality' seems to be a cover up for her awkwardness and condesention towards the poet. She is trying to remain unmoved, but the reader knows it is trying to mask the prejudice underneath. It distances the reader, the landlady is just a voice, with no feeling, trying to remain impersonal.

Soyinka uses the poem as a vehicle for confronting and challenging prejudice. There is a point in the poem before which the poet is hurt and upset by the conversation, but after which he changes tone and begins to make fun of the idiocy of the question 'How dark?'. He plays the stupidity of it by describing his feet and hands as peroxide blond, and his bottom as 'raven black'. This ironic description of himself confronts the unspoken prejudice of the landlady. We can feel her uncomfortable presence on the other end of the phone.

He finally confronts the prejudice implied throughout the poem by pleading 'wouldn't you rather see for yourself?'. He is asking to be seen as a person, rather than being dismissed over the phone. He is challenging the prejudice by making the landlady confront him and see him as a person. Once the landlady 'sees for' herself she won't be able to hide behind the telephone and a mask of impersonality. Soyinka is in effect challenging the prejudice by making fun of its triviality.

- Still working in pairs, look more closely at this exam answer and talk about how well you think the student has answered the question. Begin by underlining all the points which answer the question. Next, using a different colour, highlight any comments which are not relevant. Finally, list the points which you think the student should have included, but has missed out.

- Use the mark scheme printed below to help you write a short note to the pupil commenting on what they have done well and offering advice about how they could further improve their answer.

< D   Candidates will make a small number of simple and relevant points from the poem, and will present these with limited understanding of the situation and language.

D   Candidates will make several relevant points from the poem selected, referring to key incidents and feelings, and will present these with some understanding of language and the poem's implications but without full development or depth.

C   Candidates will make a fair number of sound points from the poem selected and present them reasonably clearly, showing some insight into the incidents selected and the language and style of the poem.

B   Candidates' responses will reveal sound analysis and interpretation of the selected poem, with clear organisation and development of the material, including a good focus on language and reasonable insight.

A   Candidates will show thoughtful analysis and sustained interpretation of the incidents and the language in the poem, and will present these coherently, in a well-organised response which shows good insight.

A*   Candidates will show an extremely assured grasp of the incidents and language of the poem, with the ability to present and analyse these with clarity and originality, and to sustain an interpretation which shows considerable penetration and insight.

The teacher's comments

- Read the teacher's comments on this essay, re-printed for you here.

You have given a sound overview of the poem, identified and explored the main ideas it raises, and expressed your own response energetically and in a clear, well-organised way. You have selected some appropriate details from the text, and integrated these effectively into your own writing. What you have not done so successfully is look closely and consistently enough at the language which the poet has chosen to use in order to show how particular words and phrases contribute to the impact of his ideas on the reader.

You note the form of the poem – a telephone conversation. Your answer traces the development of the situation which the poem describes in a way which shows your understanding of the poet's feelings and the tones in which he and the landlady speak. However, your answer mainly concentrates on the exchange between the two speakers. Your own strong response to the racism implied in the landlady's questions has distracted you from looking closely enough at how Soyinka expresses his own thoughts and feelings. Your comments in paragraph three that 'the reader and poet are shocked' and that the poet feels shame and humiliation' show insight, but need to be supported and developed by further exploration of lines 9-16. Look, for example, at the punning implications of 'public hide-and-speak' or the repetition of 'red' in line 13, or the effect of the brief impressions of smells and sights bracketed between 'I had not misheard' and 'It *was* real!'

In paragraph four, you write 'there is a point in the poem ... after which he changes tone'. Noting shifts in tone is an excellent way of exploring how a poem develops – you would be given credit for this in your exam, but being so vague about where these shifts happen is not particularly useful. The examiner, like me, is interested in where you think the shifts in tone occur, and why you think so. Paying closer attention to the language in the poem would help you to pinpoint the shift more precisely – and gain you more marks!

You show good insight into Soyinka's irony in the final nine lines of the poem. However, the ending of the essay would be strengthened by looking at how this irony is conveyed to the reader. You've noted how Soyinka draws attention to the 'idiocy' of the landlady's demand for him to be specific about his skin colour by describing his 'peroxide blonde' palms and soles, and 'raven black' bottom. You could have developed the point about irony with a comment on his mock-humble explanation that the 'raven black' bottom has been caused by his being 'foolish' enough to sit down on it! This could lead the reader to explore other possible layers of meaning in 'wouldn't you rather see for yourself?'. You rightly suggest that he is being asked to be seen as a person; could he also be returning insult for insult? What do you think?

There are some very positive features in this essay – overall understanding of the content, engagement with the ideas, strong personal response, use of textual detail as part of a clearly organised essay. Well done! You are doing all the right things. To improve your work further, you now need to work at analysing and commenting in more detail on the writer's choices and uses of language, and the effect of these.

- Compare what the teacher has written with your own advice to the student.

- Talk with your class and teacher about the grade you would give this answer. Justify your ideas by referring closely to both the mark scheme and the essay.

Achievements and targets
- Working in pairs, look back at the answers you wrote to this question. See how many of the comments about the pupil's essay apply to your own work. Use what you have learned to make a list of your achievements in this essay and to set yourself one or two targets for your next one (for example, to focus on the language of the poem as well as its content).

Big School, Big Trauma and Starting School

Both of these articles were published in *The Independent* newspaper on the same day, September 7th, 1995, the beginning of the school year.

- Before reading either article spend a few minutes brainstorming your own memories of starting secondary school. You could think about:
- the things you were worried about
- what you were looking forward to
- what happened on your first day
- the way the school tried to make the move from primary to secondary school easier
- other things you think the school should have done.

- Share your thoughts with the rest of the class.

Reading 'Big School, Big Trauma'

Talking about the title
- Talk briefly, as a class, about your response to this title. What are your expectations of the article it introduces? What do the choice of words and the structure of the headline suggest about the subject matter and the angle the writer has taken? Who do you think the intended audience is?

Reading the article
- Read the article or listen to it being read out loud. How far does it meet your expectations? In pairs, talk briefly about the aspects of the article which meet your expectations and those which surprised you.

The message to schools?

• In one sentence sum up what you think this article's message to schools is. Swap sentences in small groups and see how far you agree about your interpretations of the passage.

• As a class talk briefly about the way in which the writer, Celia Dodds, directs the response of the reader.

• Using two different coloured pens highlight the advantages (for both the pupils and the schools) of transition programmes like the one outlined here by Ted Wragg.

Exploring the style

• Make a list of the words you would use to describe the style and tone of this article, for example formal, chatty, distant, persuasive, critical and so on.

The style, tone and effect of the passage are all affected by the choices writers make. These choices can be divided into:
– the words writers use
– the way writers structure sentences
– the organisation, into a whole text, of the points writers want to make.

Use the following activities to help you focus on its language and structure.

– the structure of the passage

The article has a logical structure which helps the writer sound authoritative, adding weight to the argument she is communicating (that schools should do more to ease the transition of pupils starting secondary school). The different sections of the article are summarised below.

Introducing the subject.

Setting the subject in context.

Summarising the fears of the students.

Providing anecdotal evidence.

Providing research evidence.

Quoting the opinions of experts.

Suggesting what can be done to overcome these anxieties.

• Working in pairs identify the techniques Celia Dodds uses to link these sections and move the reader through the piece.

– sentence structures

Choose a short section from the article and examine closely the way the writer structures each sentence. For instance, does she use long sentences, linking her ideas together using the word 'and'? Have a go at re-writing one or two of Celia Dodds' sentences and comment on the effect. (For example, re-write a long sentence as a series of very short points.)

– word choices

Make a note of any word choices which you find particularly powerful or persuasive. Does the position of the word, or who it is said by, alter the effect it has on you, the reader?

– other techniques

What other techniques does Celia Dodds use to make her article seem serious, reflective and authoritative? How effective do you find techniques such as quoting people who are regarded as experts?

Reading 'Starting School'

- Read the second article and jot down your general impressions. You could organise your ideas under the following headings:
- the way the article is presented in the paper (headline, introductory paragraph)
- the way the passage is written (for example, structure and organisation; word choices and so on). You might find it helpful to highlight the things the writer is looking forward to in one colour and the things he is worried about in another. What do you notice about the relationship between these hopes and fears?

- Taking into account what you have learned from Celia Dodds' article, outline any additional things James' new school could do to help alleviate his anxieties.

An editorial decision

It is unusual for a newspaper to publish an article by a child as young as James. You are more likely to see the views of children as quotations in articles by adult writers or in the form of an interview. In this case the editor of *The Independent* not only decided to use James' own words, but to credit him with being the writer.

- Use the following headings to help you think about the issues raised here:
- the decision of the paper to use only James' words
- James' purpose for writing
- the reason the paper has published the two articles as companion pieces.

Comparing the articles

- Make a few notes on the similarities and differences between the two articles, and share these in pairs or small groups.

- On your own, make a detailed comparison of the way the two articles have been written. Use the table below to help you plan your comparison.

	Big School, Big Trauma	**Starting School**
Content		
Point of view		
Voice		
Tone (for example, reflective, convinced, argumentative, uncertain, musing, excited, confused, meandering, authoritative)		
Style and language		
Purpose/message		
The effect on the reader		

Writing/oral suggestions

1. Re-writing 'Starting School'

Use James Bateson's piece as the basis for a more formal article, written in the style of Celia Dodds' 'Big School, Big Trauma', on a pupil's experience of starting secondary school. Annotate your article to show the structural and language features which have transformed it from the style James Bateson used to that used by Celia Dodds. Have a look back at your completed table to help you do this.

2. A comparative essay

Use your notes and completed table in order to write a short comparison of the two articles. You could use the opening suggested here to help get you thinking.

Both articles tackle the subject of starting secondary school. However, whereas 'Big School, Big Trauma' is written in the third person, in a formal, objective style, 'Starting School' is .....

3. Designing a leaflet

Plan and draft a leaflet designed to inform and reassure pupils in year 6. Before you begin, look back at the brainstorm you made of your memories and the notes you have made while studying the two articles. You will need to think carefully about audience (parents? pupils? both?) and purpose (to inform? to reassure? to excite? Remember, different sections of the leaflet might have different purposes.).

The decisions you make about your purpose and audience will affect the content, language, organisation and presentation of the leaflet.
- content (facts about the school? information about school uniform? details of the first day? exciting trips pupils can look forward to?)
- organisation
- language (formal or chatty? Whichever register you choose your writing should be clear and straightforward.)
- presentation (bullet points? sub-headings? cartoons? quotations?).

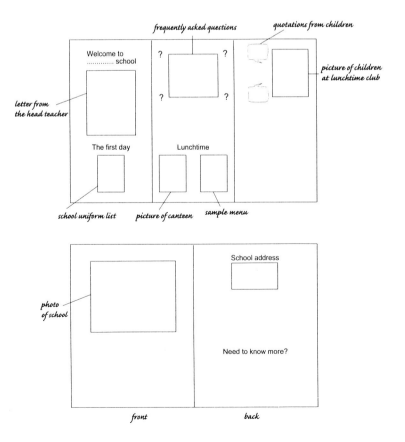

Black Boy

The final sentence
The final sentence from this passage is printed below.

> That night I won the right to the streets of Memphis

- Working on your own or with a partner, begin by jotting down all the questions this raises in your mind, for example, what happened on this particular night?

- Then, looking more closely at this same sentence, begin to jot down some notes, speculating about the following aspects of the piece:
- the character of the narrator
- the incident
- the place
- the message or theme of the passage.

Some annotations have been added to help you get started.

'the right' strange that this is something that has to be won. Isn't it something every body has the right to?

That night I won the right to the streets of Memphis

Possible reasons someone might not have the right to the streets? Does it mean the right to walk the streets? Why doesn't it say this?

A key moment
- Now read this key moment from the passage and on your own jot down your first impressions.

'Take this money, this note, and this stick,' she said. 'Go to the store and buy those groceries. If those boys bother you, then fight.'

I was baffled. My mother was telling me to fight, a thing that she had never done before.

' But I'm scared,' I said.

' Don't you come into this house until you've gotten those groceries,' she said.

' They'll beat me; they'll beat me,' I said.

' Then stay in the streets; don't come back here!'

I ran up the steps and tried to force my way past her into the house. A stinging slap came on my jaw. I stood on the sidewalk, crying.

'Please, let me wait until tomorrow,' I begged.

'No,' she said. 'Go now! If you come back into this house without those groceries, I'll whip you!'

She slammed the door and I heard the key turn in the lock. I shook with fright. I was alone upon the dark, hostile streets and gangs were after me. I had the choice of being beaten at home or away from home.

- In small groups, or as a class, share your first impressions, and talk about what you think has already happened and what is going to happen. Some of the things you should consider are suggested here:
- the sort of woman the mother seems to be
- why you think she is behaving in this way

- the character of the narrator
- the way the passage is written (for example, the dialogue, word choices the length and type of sentence).

Reading the passage

- Listen to the whole extract being read aloud and jot down your reactions. Share these in class discussion and compare what happens in the passage with your expectations of it. Do you find any aspects of it surprising or disturbing? If so, which parts and why?

- Look back at the notes you made on the way the mother treated the boy, forcing him to go out and confront the bullies. Now you have read the whole piece why do you think she behaved in this way?

The writer's purpose

In an autobiography, the writer has to focus on what he or she thinks are key moments in their life.
- In pairs, and then as a class, talk about why you think Richard Wright includes this episode in his autobiography. What do you think is the purpose of this passage?

Exploring the way *Black Boy* is written – investigating the structure

- Match the following statements to the section of the passage you think it describes most accurately.

> The climax of the story.
> Establishing background and context.
> Introducing the complication or problem.
> Developing the problem/increasing the tension.
> Setting the scene.
> The message of the story.

- What type of writing is it? On your own identify the sections which use description, commentary, dialogue or action. Then talk in pairs about how each section works. What does each contribute to the overall effect of the passage?

Developing tension

One of the key features of this extract is the way Richard Wright develops tension, communicating to the reader the anxieties of the young boy.
- As a class spend a few minutes brainstorming some words to describe the feelings of the young boy at different stages of the episode. Make a list of his worries and concerns.

- Next look back at the extract and choose a short quotation to illustrate two or three of the feelings you identified. Working in pairs talk about the ways in which you think the writer has managed to create, and then convey to the reader, how the young boy feels. What techniques does the author use instead of simply saying, for example, 'I was scared'?

- Share your analysis with the rest of the class and talk about any patterns you notice or language features which are repeated.

Close work on the writer's techniques
The following activities focus on the way Richard Wright develops tension throughout the whole text, within each sentence and through his word choices.

– text level
- As a class talk about the techniques used to build up tension throughout the text as a whole. A few techniques are suggested here to get you started:
- – repetition helps to build suspense
- – showing it from the young boy's perspective helps the reader feel his fear.

– sentence level
Some of the ways a writer can structure sentences in order to develop tension are suggested here:
- – a combination of short and simple sentences and longer sentences
- – repetition of the same sentence structure
- – balanced sentences
- – repeating the same structure within a single sentence
- – the rhythm of the sentence
- – the '–ing' form of the verb.

- Identify examples of these in the short extract re-printed below.

They closed in. In blind fear I let the stick fly, feeling it crack against a boy's skull. I swung again, lamming another skull, then another. Realising that they would retaliate if I let up for a second, I fought to lay them low, to knock them cold, to kill them so that they could not strike back at me. I flayed with tears in my eyes, teeth clenched, stark fear making me throw every ounce of my strength behind each blow. I hit again and again, dropping the money and the grocery list. The boys scattered, yelling, nursing their heads, staring at me in utter disbelief. They had never seen such a frenzy. I stood panting, egging them on, taunting them to come and fight.

- For each technique you identify, write a sentence analysing the way it works in the passage. For example,

The present participle ('–ing') form of the verb helps to create a sense of movement and action. This emphasises the powerful attack of the gang of boys.

– word level
- Now examine in more detail the ways in which the author creates a sense of tension and action through his choice of words. Underline the words which seem to be doing the work in this passage. Then group them according to the type of word they are or the job they do in the sentence.

How the passage works
- Talk about the relationship between the opening paragraph, the story of the fight and the final sentence. How do these sections work together to produce a coherent text?

Writing/oral suggestions
1. The mother's diary
In role, write the mother's diary for the night after this incident. Explain what happened and why she behaved as she did. You should also try and describe the way she felt when she made her young son repeatedly go out into the street.

2. A critical essay
Write a short critical essay commenting on the relationship between the message of the passage, its themes and purpose and the way Richard Wright has told it. Does it work using storytelling techniques to get his message across?

3. Writing about a key moment
Use this passage as a model for writing about a key moment like this in your own life. You should try to experiment with some of the techniques used by Richard Wright.

- Choose an incident which you think has had a profound affect on your life. This could be a happy, sad or frightening experience – it doesn't matter.
- Before you begin to write, experiment with different ways of ending your story. The final sentence is vital.
- Use repetition carefully to build up suspense and increase the reader's sense of anticipation.
- Develop tension by using a variety of sentence structures (for example, very short sentences or longer sentences made up of short clauses to convey a sense of panic). Look back at the work you did on exploring the writer's techniques for other ideas.
- Use dialogue between the characters to create a sense of drama.
- Choose your verbs carefully. Look back at the verbs Richard Wright used to describe the fight scene, for example, fought, knock, kill, flayed, clenched and yelled.

Fenland Chronicle

'Fenland Chronicle' is taken from a compilation of first person accounts and recollections of life in Norfolk during the early part of the twentieth century. The narrator of the piece is not a professional writer: her story is an example of an oral history, spoken aloud, recorded and now written down.

First impressions
- Listen to the piece being read aloud and make some brief notes on your first response. Concentrate on recording your impressions of the following features:
- the character of the narrator
- what you learn about the life of a maid
- the way the story is told
- your own reactions.

Life in service
- Working in pairs, and without looking back at the passage, brainstorm everything you have learned about the life of a maid.

Sorting out the facts from the opinions
- Re-read the passage and use two different coloured pens to highlight the facts/information in one colour and the opinions in another.

- What do the opinions add to the effect of the passage?

The farmer's view
- Now you have sorted out the facts from the opinions, present the farmer's view of a young girl's life in service.

The voice of the narrator
One of the main ways in which the experiences of the young girls comes alive for the reader is through the voice of the narrator.

- How would you describe the tone of the passage? Is it, for example, chatty, confiding, argumentative? Does the tone remain the same throughout the piece or does it change according to the subject? Skim read the passage again, jotting down shifts in tone in the margin.

- Now choose one paragraph which you find particularly interesting and prepare a reading for performance. Annotate your copy with ideas on tone, pace, expression, emphasis and so on.

- Practise reading your paragraph out loud. You should aim to develop an engaging performance which reveals the character of the speaker.

Looking at language
One of the consequences of presenting this memory in the voice of the narrator is the use of dialect and non-standard English.

- Choose a short section of text and annotate it in the way shown below, highlighting the language features which you find particularly interesting.

written how it would be said (accent) - gives the reader an idea of her character

> In my opinion, good service in a properly run big house were a wonderful training for a lot o'girls who would never ha' seen anything different all the days o'their lives if they ha'n't a gone.

- Pull out three examples of dialect words and expressions and re-write each in standard English.

Dialect	Standard English	Comment on the change

- In pairs talk about what you think the use of dialect and non-standard English adds to this account of a maid's life.

The organisation of the passage
Although this is a personal memory using anecdotes, it is not unstructured.
- Read the passage again and divide the passage into sections. Compare your divisions with other people in your class, explaining why you have divided it in this way. Once you have agreed on the main sections of the passage, write a sentence explaining what each one is about and what you think is most distinctive about its style.

Writing/oral suggestions
1. A job description
Use the facts you have identified to write a job description. Your purpose is to inform a young girl of the duties, responsibilities and daily life she can expect. You should also include details of the working and living conditions and payment. Try not to let any opinions creep in. You could begin with a paragraph summarising the job, then list the girl's work routine. Use sub-headings to help you organise your writing.

2. A historian speaks: 'Girls in service'
As a first person recollection 'Fenland Chronicle' is very valuable for someone trying to piece together what life was like at the time. Turn it into a formal lecture, using quotations from the anecdotes as evidence for your comments. You could use this structure to help organise your talk:
- a description of what being in service meant
- the advantages of being in service
- the experiences of the girls in the fens
- general points about working conditions
- an example of the daily routine of a maid
- some views of the girls who worked in service.

3. Reviewing 'Fenland Chronicle'
Imagine you are a reviewer for a magazine called *Norfolk Memories*. This month you have decided to write a piece on 'Fenland Chronicle' considering both the content and style. Use the headings suggested below to structure your piece:
- an overview of the piece (what it is about, the point of view, the style)
- a summary of the life described
- the character of the narrator
- the opinions expressed
- the way in which the experiences are brought to life
- the structure of the piece
- an evaluation of whether or not you think this is an effective way of telling stories about the past and why.

Notes from a Small Island – prologue

Before reading

- In small groups talk about the first thoughts, feelings and visual images you have when you hear the word England, for example cold and rainy. Next, talk about the images and stereotypes which people from other countries seem to have of England, for example, men in bowler hats. In note-form summarise the main points of your discussion.

Looking at the title

- Look carefully at the title *Notes From a Small Island*. Jot down all the things it suggests about the type of book this extract is taken from. You could think about the following points to help focus your ideas:
- – content
- – style
- – genre
- – tone.

- Write a paragraph outlining what you think the prologue will be about.

Reading the passage

- Listen to the passage being read aloud making a note of your response in the margin. How does the passage compare with your expectations?

Purpose and audience

- Listed below are some of the aims Bill Bryson may have had when writing the prologue to *Notes From a Small Island*.

- To tell a story.
- To make fun of the English.
- To inform people what England is like.
- To establish the character of the narrator.
- To make fun of himself.
- To show how wonderful England is.

- Choose the purposes which you think are most important in this extract and add any of your own. Then find examples from the text to illustrate each one.

- After sharing your ideas about the purpose for writing, spend some time thinking about the type of person you think this book would appeal to.

- Very quickly skim read the passage again and jot down some of the sections or features which you think would attract the type of reader you have identified.

An image of the narrator

In this passage readers learn as much about the narrator as they do about the town of Dover and its inhabitants.
- Jot down your own impressions of the narrator, Bill Bryson. Find evidence in the passage for these impressions and share these with the rest of the class.

Investigating the structure

- Read the extract again, making a mark every time you think Bill Bryson moves on to a new subject.

- Write an attention grabbing sub-heading for each of the sections you have identified.

- Feedback these sub-headings in class discussion and talk about what it tells you about the structure of the passage.

Looking at style – humour

Notes From a Small Island does not just inform the reader about the places Bryson visits and the people he meets as he travels round England. It is also very funny. Some of the features which make the book amusing are listed here:
- the difference between Bryson's expectations and the reality
- exaggeration
- stereotypes (we recognise the type of people he describes)
- laughing at himself
- humorous comparisons
- painting vivid visual pictures
- the absurd.

- Choose two or three of these features and for each one pick out a short section of the text where you think it is used effectively. Join up with another person and explain why the techniques you have chosen are particularly funny.

Looking at language – tone

Listed below are a number of adjectives used to describe writing styles.
- Choose the three words which you think describe most accurately the style of the passage and identify a quotation from the passage to illustrate each. Use a dictionary to clarify the meanings of any words you haven't come across before.

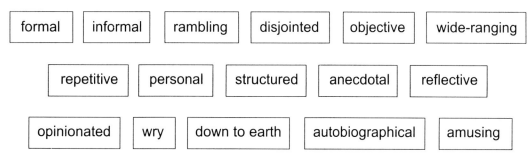

| formal | informal | rambling | disjointed | objective | wide-ranging |

| repetitive | personal | structured | anecdotal | reflective |

| opinionated | wry | down to earth | autobiographical | amusing |

- Now you have analysed in more detail the style of Bill Bryson's writing, look back at the purposes for writing which you identified in the passage. Talk about the ways in which the style of writing is suitable for the purpose.

Reading the reviews

- Read through the selection of reviews of *Notes From A Small Island*, thinking about the comments which seem to you most apt.

> Splendid ... What's enjoyable is that there's as much of Bryson in here as there is of Britain. (*Sunday Telegraph*)

> Bryson is funny because he is not afraid to give of himself completeiy. (*Daily Express*)

> Laugh-out-loud funny (*Good Book Guide*)

> Not a book that should be read in public, for fear of emitting loud snorts (*The Times*)

- Use these quotations from the reviews to spark off ideas for writing your own review of *Notes From a Small Island*.

- Spend a few minutes in groups or as a class listening to each other's reviews. Talk about the similarities and differences in people's evaluation of the passage.

Writing/oral suggestions
1. The next chapter
Imagine Bill Bryson visits the town you live in. Imitate the style he uses in the prologue and write a short article commenting on the people, places and customs.
Then write a commentary to go with this, describing the effects you were trying to achieve and the techniques you used to do this.

2. Notes from ...
This passage recounts in a humorous tone Bill Bryson's first impressions of England. It contrasts his high expectations with the cold reality.
Spend a few minutes noting down some of the places you have visited which have not lived up to your expectations. Choose the place you have most vivid memories of, or which you remember as particularly disappointing, and develop your notes into a short description, using some of the techniques used in *Notes From a Small Island* in order to interest and entertain your reader.

3. Selling the book
Using the notes you have made on purpose, audience and style write a short blurb to publicise *Notes From a Small Island*. You should make sure you emphasise those aspects of the book you think will attract the type of reader you are focusing on.

Seize the Moment

Before reading
- Spend a few minutes brainstorming likely thoughts and feelings of someone preparing to go into space for the first time. Share these as a class before listening to the passage being read aloud.

An autobiography – reading the writer
You can learn a lot about someone from the way they react to events, what they choose to focus on and how they talk about the experience.
- Bearing this in mind, jot down your impression of Helen Sharman. Justify your ideas by analysing and commenting on short sections of this account of her first trip into space.

Purpose and audience
Who do you think this is aimed at? What do you think the purpose is? How can you tell?
- Look at the list of statements about the passage and choose the three which you think describe, most accurately, the writer's purpose in this passage.

- To record her experiences for history.
- To capture in language the wonder and beauty of the experience.
- To help the public understand what it is like to go into space.
- To teach people about what is involved in space travel.
- To teach people about the science of space travel.
- To tell a story.
- To interest the general reader.
- To interest the expert.
- To make the reader think.

- For each statement you choose write a few sentences explaining your choice. You should include short quotations to illustrate the points you make.

- Is there anything about the account which you find surprising? Or has anything been missed out that you expected to see there?

Looking at the structure
- On your own, divide the passage into sections. Compare your sections with your partner and talk about what influenced your decisions. As a whole class come up with a way of dividing the passage into sections that you are all happy with. Talk about which of the following statements seems the most appropriate way of describing the structure.

- It is chronological.
- It is logical.
- It is poetic.
- It is structured by association.

The talisman
- In her description of the launch and the spacecraft's entry into space Helen Sharman refers on several occasions to the 'talisman'. Find out what a 'talisman' is. Talk about how it is used in this piece:
- as a way of structuring the passage
- to indicate the different stages of the take-off
- to tell us something about what Helen Sharman feels about the launch
- as a metaphor.

Looking at language – tone

* Skim read the passage again, making a mark each time you think there is a shift in the tone. Now look at the list of words printed below and choose the ones you think describe most accurately the different sections of *Seize the Moment*.

| chatty | conversational | poetic | dramatic | excited |

| reflective | scientific | precise | matter of fact | detailed |

Looking at language – a unique experience

• Working in groups look more closely at the way Helen Sharman uses language to convey the experiences. Each group should take responsibility for exploring one of the language groups suggested here.

• For each example you find, analyse the effect of using the particular word or phrase and comment on the contribution this type of language makes to the overall piece.

Language group	Example	Comment
specialist		
descriptive		
metaphoric		
personal		
emotional		
technical (including facts and figures)		

* Next get into new groups. Each new group should have at least one person from each of the original groups. Take turns to report back your group's discussion of the language of *Seize the Moment*.

* As a class talk about your discoveries (for example, why you think so much specialist language is used) and your evaluations of this language use (for example, what it contributes to the experience of reading this autobiography).

Developing tension

* Working on your own, investigate the techniques Sharman uses to reflect the build up of tension as the shuttle is launched and enters space. Some ideas have been given to get you started. For each one, find an example of where this technique is used and comment on its effect in the passage. The first one has been done for you.

– She uses short sentences *to make a dramatic point, for example, 'sunlight streamed in. I looked down at the earth. We were already over the Pacific.'*
– She repeats sentence structures ...
– She uses exclamations ...

Writing/oral suggestions
1. Interviewing the astronaut

Imagine you are going to interview Helen Sharman, first for *Newsround* and then for *News at Ten*. Come up with a list of questions you would ask in each case. Although some will be common to both interviews, you will need to think carefully about the different audience for the interviews. Think about the different questions you would ask. Then based on the information in the piece jot down the answers you think she would give.

Working in pairs you could take it in turns to answer these questions in role.

2. Women on the Edge – a magazine article

Imagine you are a writer in the features department of a best-selling women's magazine. As part of a series called 'Women on the Edge' you have decided to write a piece on Helen Sharman. Some of the things you need to think about are listed below:

– purpose
– audience
– what difference it makes to write in the third rather than first person
– the tone you use
– the inclusion of quotation or other references to authority
– presentation, including pictures and diagrams.

Compare your magazine article with the original text of the autobiography and comment on the differences in presentation, structure and style.

3. A critical essay

Write in detail about the experience Helen Sharman describes in *Seize the Moment*. You should comment on the writing techniques used to re-create this experience and the effect of the descriptions on the reader. Use the following headings to help you organise your ideas:

– your response
– Helen Sharman's purpose
– what she focuses on
– the tone
– the relationship with the reader
– type of language used/word choice
– the sentence structures
– the organisation and structure of the whole passage.